Pebble Plus

Cool Sports Facts

Cool BMX Racing Facts

by Sandy Donovan

Consulting Editor: Gail Saunders-Smith, PhD

Consultants: Keith Mulligan, Editor in Chief
Ride BMX / TransWorld Media
and
Fat Tony, Online Editor
ridebmx.com / TransWorld Media

CAPSTONE PRESS
a capstone imprint

Pebble Plus is published by Capstone Press,
1710 Roe Crest Drive, North Mankato, Minnesota 56003.
www.capstonepub.com

Copyright © 2011 by Capstone Press, a Capstone imprint. All rights reserved.
No part of this publication may be reproduced in whole or in part, or stored in a retrieval system, or transmitted in any form or by any means, electronic, mechanical, photocopying, recording, or otherwise, without written permission of the publisher. For information regarding permission, write to Capstone Press,
1710 Roe Crest Drive, North Mankato, Minnesota 56003.

Library of Congress Cataloging-in-Publication Data
Donovan, Sandra, 1967–
  Cool BMX racing facts / by Sandy Donovan.
    p. cm. — (Pebble plus. Cool sports facts)
  Includes bibliographical references and index.
  Summary: "Simple text and full-color photos illustrate facts about the history, equipment, tricks, and records of BMX racing"—Provided by publisher.
  ISBN 978-1-4296-5304-6 (library binding)
  ISBN 978-1-4296-6204-8 (paperback)
  ISBN 978-1-4296-8761-4 (saddle-stitch)
  1. Bicycle motocross—Juvenile literature. I. Title. II. Series.
GV1049.3.D67 2011
796.6'2—dc22   2010028899

Editorial Credits
Katy Kudela, editor; Kyle Grenz, designer; Eric Gohl, media researcher; Laura Manthe, production specialist

Photo Credits
Alamy/Niels Poulsen DK, 17
Bruce Mulligan, 9
Getty Images Inc./AFP/Carl de Souza, 21; Craig Dutton, 11; UCI/Angel Martinez, 15; UCI/Michael Steele, cover, 13
iStockphoto/dd72, cover (bicycle), back cover, 1
Scot "OM" Breithaupt, 7
Shutterstock/Timothy Large, 5
Tim Lillethorup, 19

Every effort has been made to contact copyright holders of any materials reproduced in this book. Any omission will be rectified in subsequent printings if notice is given to the publishers.

Note to Parents and Teachers

The Cool Sports Facts series supports national social studies standards related to people, places, and culture. This book describes and illustrates BMX racing. The images support early readers in understanding the text. The repetition of words and phrases helps early readers learn new words. This book also introduces early readers to subject-specific vocabulary words, which are defined in the Glossary section. Early readers may need assistance to read some words and to use the Table of Contents, Glossary, Read More, Internet Sites, and Index sections of the book.

Printed in China.
092011   006411

Table of Contents

Extreme Biking........ 4
Cool History 6
Cool Equipment 10
Cool Racing Skills .. 14
Cool Records 18

Glossary 22
Read More........... 23
Internet Sites 23
Index 24

Extreme Biking

BMX is fun to do and watch.

But pay attention!

Some races are finished

in less than 40 seconds.

BMX stands for bicycle motocross.

5

Cool History

BMX races started out small. In 1970 Scot Breithaupt held a race for 30 children. The next week, 150 children were lined up to race.

Scot Breithaupt

By the 1980s BMX had grown into a national sport. People watched races on TV. BMX racing was in movies like *Rad*.

9

Cool Equipment

BMX bikes speed over dirt tracks.

BMX bikes have wide, thick tires.

Grooves and knobbies on the tires grip the dirt tracks.

11

Riders must beware of crashes.

To stay safe, they wear

full-face helmets.

A full-face helmet covers a

rider's head and mouth.

13

Cool Racing Skills

BMX racers use tricks to help their speed. Before the race they "balance on the gate." They stand on their pedals to get going faster.

15

In a heated race, a BMX racer can do a manual. The racer gains speed by rolling over a jump on the back wheel.

17

Cool Records

Dave Clinton is known for his speed and his tabletop trick. In 1985 he became the first member of the BMX Hall of Fame.

Dave Clinton

In 2008 BMX racing came to the Olympics. Maris Strombergs won the men's gold medal. Anne-Caroline Chausson won the women's gold medal.

Maris Strombergs

Glossary

BMX Hall of Fame—a group of racers, freestyle riders, and other people who are important to BMX

gate—a long metal frame that racers start on; gates drop down at the beginning of a race

groove—a long cut in the surface of something

helmet—a hard hat that protects your head during sports or dangerous activities

knobbie—a rounded bump on a tire

pedal—a lever on a bicycle that you push with your foot

tabletop—a jumping trick where the rider lays the bike flat in the air

track—a path or a trail

Read More

Blomquist, Christopher. *BMX in the X Games.* A Kid's Guide to the X Games. New York: PowerKids Press, 2003.

David, Jack. *BMX Racing.* Action Sports. Minneapolis: Bellwether Media, 2008.

Internet Sites

FactHound offers a safe, fun way to find Internet sites related to this book. All of the sites on FactHound have been researched by our staff.

Here's all you do:

Visit www.facthound.com

Type in this code: 9781429653046

Check out projects, games and lots more at www.capstonekids.com

Index

BMX Hall of Fame, 18
Breithaupt, Scot, 6
Chausson, Anne-Caroline, 20
Clinton, Dave, 18
crashes, 12
helmets, 12
jumps, 16

Olympic Games, 20
racing moves, 14, 16
Rad (movie), 8
safety, 12
Strombergs, Maris, 20
tires, 10, 16
tracks, 10
tricks, 14, 18

Word Count: 204
Grade: 1
Early-Intervention Level: 20